HOW TO DEAL WITH DIFFICULT PEOPLE

Other titles available from SkillPath Publications, Inc.:

The Supervisor's Guide

Power Write! A Practical Guide to Words that Work

Every Woman's Guide to Career Success

Taking Charge: A Personal Guide to Managing
    Projects and Priorities

Meetings That Work

*Hiring and Firing: What Every Manager Needs to
    Know*

HOW TO DEAL WITH DIFFICULT PEOPLE

Paul G. Friedman, Ph.D.

SkillPath Publications, Inc.
Mission, Kansas

Copyeditor: Kelly Scanlon

ISBN 1-878542-03-6

Printed in the United States of America

CONTENTS

Introduction 1

What Makes People Difficult? 3
    Exercise 1: Your People Network 3
    Exercise 2: Problems and Goals with Difficult People 5

Changing Difficult Behavior 11
    Exercise 3: Blaming Patterns 14
    Exercise 4: Analyzing the Problem 15

Preventing Difficulties 21
    Exercise 5: Preventing Difficulties 37

Being The Solution, Not The Problem 39
    Exercise 6: Self-Annihilating Games 49

Difficult Modes of Talk 53
    Exercise 7: Communication Modes 55

Encouraging Desirable Behavior 61
    Exercise 8: Tracking Positives 63
    Exercise 9: Messages of Praise 67
    Exercise 10: Conditioned Appreciation Messages 69

Summing It Up 71

INTRODUCTION

Management expert Peter Drucker once wryly remarked, "Working with people is difficult, but not impossible." That's also a basic thesis of this book. It's certainly obvious that many people are "difficult" to deal with, but after reading this book, you won't find them "impossible." You'll be empowered to understand behavior patterns better and establish good working relationships with even the most frustrating of individuals.

To be genuinely useful, this book should be personally practical. It is filled with information that

- helps you understand why difficult people do what they do
- provides guidelines for making progress toward achieving your specific goals

As new information is introduced, you should highlight, underline or bracket ideas that you can use when dealing with the difficult people you encounter. It will be most valuable if you apply the material directly and immediately to your interaction with specific people you currently deal with at work.

Exercises are inserted periodically to help you put the ideas in this book to use. By applying these skills, you should see a definite improvement in your interpersonal relations.

HOW TO DEAL WITH DIFFICULT PEOPLE

WHAT MAKES
PEOPLE DIFFICULT?

IDENTIFYING DIFFICULT PEOPLE

Let's get off to a flying start with an exercise for identifying
the difficult person(s) in your life. Begin by thinking of all the
people you deal with regularly in the course of a typical day.
Exercise 1 consists of a chart on which you can quickly map
your "people network." Think of yourself as being in the
center. Each of the peripheral circles represents one of the
people with whom you interact. Fill in their names (just their
initials will do). You needn't use every circle, and you can add
more circles if you wish to include more people. You also
might put a *group* of people in a circle — the accounting
department, impatient customers, etc.).

✍ Exercise 1: Your People Network

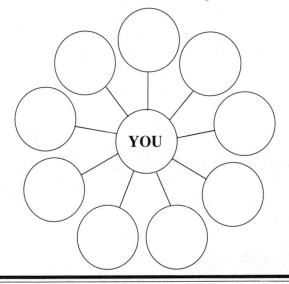

Next assess the degree to which you have difficulty dealing with each of the people on your chart. Mentally review your recent interactions with each person. Sense within yourself the degree to which you are satisfied with that relationship. On the line that connects your circle with theirs, indicate the degree of satisfaction or "difficulty" you experience.

• Use angular diagonals to indicate the people with whom you experience difficulty.
• Use smooth curving lines to indicate the people with whom your interaction is satisfactory.

Below is an example of some difficulty indicators:

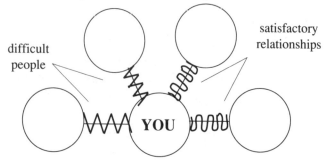

This diagram now reveals at a glance the people with whom you have most difficulty and those with whom you communicate best. You can learn a lot by analyzing both kinds of relationships.

DESCRIBING DIFFICULT PEOPLE

The next step in self-awareness calls for specifying a few things the most difficult people in your life do or don't do. These descriptions provide a clear definition of the problem situation(s) you are facing. It is important, too, to specify exactly what you would prefer those people to do. Identifying what you want provides clear target(s) to shoot for (see Exercise 2).

Describing difficult people usually is more elusive than naming them. It's not easy to express in words what people do that bothers us, or what we would prefer that they do.

✍ Exercise 2: Problems and Goals with Difficult People

1. a.   A behavior I find *difficult* to handle is _____

   _____

   _____

   b.   I *wish* that person would _____

   _____

   _____

2. a.   A behavior I find *difficult* to handle is _____

   _____

   _____

   b.   I *wish* that person would _____

   _____

   _____

3. a.   A behavior I find *difficult* to handle is _____

   _____

   _____

   b.   I *wish* that person would _____

   _____

   _____

DIFFICULT TYPES

In his well-known book *Coping with Difficult People*, psychologist Robert Bramson identifies several types of difficult people.[1] Compare his typology to the difficult people with whom you deal:

Hostile-Aggressives bully and overwhelm by bombarding others, making cutting remarks or throwing tantrums when situations don't go the way such people are certain they should.

Complainers gripe incessantly but never do anything to resolve what they complain about.

Silent and unresponsives respond to every question and every plea for help with a yes, a no or a grunt.

Super-Agreeables are very reasonable, sincere and supportive in the presence of others but don't produce what they say they will, or they act contrary to the way they have led others to expect.

Negativists object "It won't work" or "It's impossible" when a project is proposed. All too often they deflate any optimism others might have.

Know-It-All Experts are "superior" people who believe and want others to recognize that they know everything there is to know about anything worth knowing. Such people are condescending, imposing (if they really do know what they're talking about) or pompous (if they don't), and they often make others feel like idiots.

Indecisives stall major decisions until the decisions are made for them. They can't let go of anything until it is perfect–which means never.

Did you find your difficult people in Bramson's typology? One shortcoming of his list is that it categorizes and labels people. Many people prefer, however, to speak about what's difficult in terms of specific behaviors or incidents, rather than to refer to particular kinds of people. Every day each of us does something that someone finds difficult. But that doesn't make us all "difficult people."

CATEGORIES OF DIFFICULT BEHAVIOR

Communication researchers Craig Monroe, Mark Borzoi and Vincent DiSalvo define difficult behavior as what people do *despite corrective feedback from their employer.* Everyone does some things that irk other people. But most people desist or change when told that their behavior is irritating or inappropriate. The researchers say the behavior of truly difficult employees must be "a constant source of problems, despite feedback designed to correct the difficult behavior."[2] They asked 381 managers, from nine widely varying organizations, to think of one male and one female subordinate who fit this definition and to describe a recent example of their behavior. The managers' responses were divided into these four categories of difficult behavior:

Apparent Compliance (mentioned by 40%). The subordinate appears to accept negative feedback from a superior, promises to change and then reverts back to his or her typical pattern of difficult behavior.

"If I've told _____ once, I've told her a thousand times, to check the procedure manual before filling out requisitions. She always apologizes all over herself and promises to do it next time. She continues to goof up. I swear she just doesn't listen."

Discouraging Word (mentioned by 21%). The subordinate refuses to accept the superior's feedback.

"_____ has been with this agency for 25 years. In the seven years I've been here, he has criticized every change we've tried to make. His standard line with me and the others is 'When you have been here as long as I have, you'll learn that this kind of thing won't work.' I respect his experience, but I'm tired of being made to feel like a snot-nosed kid."

Alibis (mentioned by 20%). The subordinate transfers responsibility for problems elsewhere. For example:

"My assistant manager knows he is responsible for managing inventory. It's in his job description. Whenever I mention it to him, though, he has an excuse: 'I'm tired or I'm overworked or that should be _____'s job.' I'm sick of it."

Avoidance (mentioned by 19%). The subordinate absents him- or herself from the scene.
"When trouble arises, _____ can't be found. One time last year he took two weeks of sick leave right after his performance appraisal. I guess he may have been sick, but this is typical of him. I doubt it."

> *"We use a lot of memos in this company. I have a file full of the ones I've sent to _____. The kid has a lot of potential if she would just follow procedure. She hasn't responded to me yet."*

Clearly, many people besides yourself face some basic forms of difficult behavior. Note that the difficult behaviors stated in the examples could occur in *any* organization. None were profession-specific or position-specific. Human relations problems crop up wherever people must work together. As Theodore Houser once wrote, "It's not the hundred-and-one problems of production and distribution that keep executives awake at night; it's the problems of working with people, the human problems of their job." Focusing attention on difficult behaviors, specifying what they are, and identifying how they might be changed—as you have in this chapter—are key steps in handling them.

ENDNOTES

1. Robert M. Bramson, *Coping with Difficult People* (New York: Ballantine Books, 1981).

2. Craig Monroe, Mark Borzoi, and Vincent DiSalvo, "Conflict Behaviors of Difficult Subordinates," *The Southern Communication Journal* 54 (4/89): 311-329.

CHANGING DIFFICULT BEHAVIOR

You can do a lot to influence the people around you. Before labeling someone "difficult," it's only fair to be sure you've done your best to change that person's behavior. The person could simply be oblivious to your discontent or underestimate it and assume you really don't mind. Changing someone's behavior involves several factors.

FRAMING THE PROBLEM

One factor you must analyze is how you "frame" the problem. The way you think about and describe a problem affects how people respond to it. The greatest danger is simply imposing your own "cause-effect" sequence on what has occurred. Behavior occurs in an ongoing stream–"life is just one darn thing after another" as the saying goes. People impose on that stream their own interpretations of what is "cause" and what is "effect."

Recall the example of the worker in the first chapter who didn't fill out requisition forms correctly. Her boss is likely to assume she is responsible for her own performance (and of course say she is). The worker might justifiably claim, however, that the procedures manual is confusing (she has a point). The writer of the procedures manual believes the instructions are clear if people are given hands-on training (oh, so that's the real cause). The training manager might say the employee was trained properly but must complete too many bureaucratic, red-tape forms and, therefore, is forced to neglect the requisitions form (aha, now we've uncovered the really real cause). The division manager might say that all the company's forms are absolutely necessary and that the problem lies with the worker's immediate boss, who is being too critical and impatient in his feedback to the worker (now we've returned to where we started). Obviously, we could go on and on, adding other possible causes and effects.

Could all of these explanations be correct? They could be.

If so, who must change to solve the problem? Any one of the parties mentioned could make a difference. Each person and procedure is an element in a sy*stem*, and each affects the others. Change in any one element will change what's occurring in the system. If this is so, no one element is exclusively at fault; none is the cause, none is the effect. No one person should be labeled the villain, no one the victim. All can be viewed as either cause or effect; all may be deemed involved and "responsible." All are possible avenues for change.

What does this "system analysis" imply about changing difficult behavior?

First, it should guide your thinking about the purpose of a change process. It's not for blaming and labeling. It *is* for identifying

- the dysfunctional system
- the elements of the system that could be affecting the difficult behavior
- alternative actions that might alter the system
- likely consequences of each action

- the action most likely to have the desired impact
- how to carry out that action

Second, it minimizes the likelihood that someone will feel hurt, angry or embarrassed when discussing the situation or that you and the difficult person will become embroiled in a debate. Bitter feelings and conflict usually arise only when dealing with a difficult person is viewed as a struggle for supremacy, for determining who will win and who will lose, for identifying who is right and who is wrong. When you eliminate accusations, you reduce the emotional upset of both parties.

Third, reframing the cause-effect model can help you involve the difficult person in handling the problem. You may view people as the "cause" of their own difficult behavior. But as we saw in the "alibi" category in the first chapter, many people project cause outward and may even see you as the "cause" and themselves in the "effect" position. If so, they're likely to place responsibility for what they're doing and the need for change on you. If you view the problem from a cause-effect frame, you'll feel resentful and debate their claim.

Rather than dispute who is at fault, you're better off if you simply acknowledge that things aren't going as they should and then ask:

- How *should* things be run?
- What can *each of us* do to bring that about?

People are more likely to carry out whatever plans are made if they themselves are involved in determining what is decided.

✍ Exercise 3: Blaming Patterns

Consider how you are framing the behaviors you find difficult.
Think of any difficult behavior you listed in Exercise 2. Then
say aloud all four of the sentences below.

1. I am to blame for _____ (the difficult behavior).
2. He (or she) is to blame for _____.
3. We both are to blame for _____.
4. No one is to blame for _____.

Which sentence do you believe is (a) most true, (b) most
satisfying to you and (c) most conducive to constructive
dialogue about the problem?_____

******

SITUATION—TARGET—PLAN

Changing someone's difficult behavior involves bridging a
gap—the discrepancy between what is occurring now, the
current *situation*, and what is preferred, the *target* —by
devising a p*lan* to facilitate that change. By formulating the
statements in Exercise 2, you've already taken the first step in
identifying the situation. However, as we've just discussed, no
situation is ever an island unto itself. All behavior is embedded
in a system, or "real-world" context.

For example, the situation has a *history*. Have previous
attempts been made to resolve the situation? In addition, you
and the other persons involved also have *limits* on what you are
willing and able to do to resolve the difficult behavior. How
much time, resources or authority do each of you have at your

disposal? What *forces* keep the person in his or her current mode of behavior? You must consider such questions when handling difficult people.

The next exercise presents a set of basic questions you must answer before devising a plan to handle any situation.

✍ Exercise 4: Analyzing the Problem

Think about the problem behavior you identified in Exercise 3 and check the appropriate answers in the spaces provided here. Your answers will guide you in developing an appropriate plan to handle the problem.

1. Does the difficult person have the *ability* to achieve the goal? Could that person, if his or her life depended on it, reach the target?   Yes ___   No ___

   The question of ability determines whether the difficult behavior is an issue of mo*tivation* (has the ability) or *skill* (lacks the ability).

2. If the answer to Question 1 is "yes," ask:
   (a) Is achieving the target specifically *rewarded*?
         Yes ___   No ___

   If you answered "no," a plan for changing the situation is now evident—you should provide *clear* and *positive consequences* for achieving the target.

   If you answered "yes," go on to item b to determine another reason.

    (b) Does achieving the target bring *negative consequences*? Yes ___   No ___

        Or is *not* achieving it rewarded?
        Yes ___   No ___

Sometimes people are criticized by their peers for going along with what the boss wants, or they fear that doing more work will cost them their job. Both of these are negative consequences for doing better work.

If your answer to either of the questions in item b is "yes," your plan should be to *improve or alter the consequences that follow achieving the target.* For example, you might separate the person from the people who discourage doing better work or relieve the person's concern that improvements could bring penalties.

3. If your answer to Question 1 was "no," ask:
    (a) Has the person ever reached the target *before*?
        Yes ___ No ___

If the answer is "no," the person needs tr*aining*.

If the answer is "yes," ask these two questions:

    (b) Does the person perform the target behavior incorrectly?   Yes ___ No ___

If the answer is "yes," the person needs *constructive feedback.*

    (c) Has the person performed the target behavior recently?
        Yes ___ No ___

If the answer is "no," the person needs *practice.*

You can see from Exercise 4, how important it is to understand fully the current situation before devising a plan for achieving the target.

The target statement you wrote in Exercise 2 is only a start toward remedying the difficult behavior. The target must be something that *both* you and the difficult person view as desirable. If you're the only one who wants to achieve the target, you'll meet resistance all along the way. As long as a person feels frustrated, coerced or required to "sacrifice" to accomplish the target, some resentment will linger and grow, eventually undermining the entire effort.

Hence, the target statement must include factors that allow everyone to feel satisfied. This has been called a "win/win" solution. Let's go back to the difficult person (a salesman) in the first chapter who predicted that every change proposed by his younger boss would fail. The boss might set a target of getting the salesman "to agree to back up his new program ideas." That would be a "win" solution for the boss. However, the salesman, who truly feels pessimistic about his boss's changes, would regard this target as a "loss" and agree to it only under duress. How could the manager set a target that *both* would regard as a win?

He would try to devise a target that takes into account the salesman's concern. The salesman thinks that anything different than the status quo is doomed to failure. The target, then, would have to include that concern as a possibility rather than to rule it out. It also would have to include the manager's optimism about his program suggestions so he feels like a "winner" too. A mutually satisfactory, win/win goal might be that "both manager and salesman agree to cooperate in a trial run of the next new program idea to see whether it works."

This is a target to which both parties might agree without feeling a "loss."

Such a target is specific and can be measured reasonably. It would be even better to identify in concrete terms what "cooperate" means and to set a specific date for assessing achievement of the target.

The plan includes the precise steps or the path to be followed when moving from the situation to the target. Often there are many alternatives for achieving a target. Hence it makes sense to explore several approaches and not simply adopt the first one that comes to mind. Nor should you commit too soon to any one way of doing things. When reviewing a possible plan, ask yourself whether

- it is likely to achieve the target
- it is practical (is the plan viable within the constraints of the situation)
- the people affected by the plan are willing and even excited about carrying it out

As mentioned previously, it is helpful to involve the "difficult person" in developing the plan. Ask the person to devise the plan or to choose a plan from two or three that are acceptable to you. Involving the "difficult person" in the choice usually elicits from that person a greater commitment to carrying out the plan successfully.

Once the plan is established, each person must understand clearly what he or she has agreed to do, by *when* and in what *form*. Checkpoints should be included along the way to ensure that the plan is being implemented as agreed. Sometimes the issue to be resolved when discussing a difficult behavior is not *what to do* but *who is to perform* a function. If this is the case, consider a process, developed by the Federal Mediation and Conciliation Service, called Relationship by Objectives (RBO). RBO is most useful when two parties disagree as to what each is supposed to do.

The first step involves having each person list (either orally or in writing) four different sets of activities:

1. I think I should . . .
2. You think you should . . .
3. I think you should . . .
4. You think I should . . .

Try to phrase your statements positively rather than negatively ("He should stop doing . . . " becomes "He should start doing . . .").

Next, working together, condense the two lists into one—the activities on which you both can agree. Pick the goals you believe deserve the highest priority and decide how to achieve them. Outline, step by step, what has to be done, when each step should be accomplished and who will be responsible for seeing it through.

To understand how this method might be applied in a specific situation, recall any instance from the past when you and someone else (a "difficult person") disagreed about the assignment of tasks—that is, when one of you felt taken advantage of, overburdened or imposed upon.

Then carry out the RBO process yourself, filling in what you think you and the other person thought each should do at the time. Recall how you actually handled the situation. Then

consider how much better your interaction would have been—
how much freer of difficulties—had you used this simple
process.

Following the full Situation—Target—Plan procedure assures
you've done your part to change the "difficult person."

PREVENTING DIFFICULTIES

DIFFERENCES VS. DIFFICULTIES

If you and I thought and acted alike, we'd never have any difficulties between us. We'd operate in perfect harmony. Difficulties arise only among people who see the world and tackle problems *differently*. Many people, therefore, try to surround themselves with similar, like-minded, agreeable people. Avoid differences and you avoid difficulties. Right?

Perhaps. But when you shun differences, you also lose a lot. Differences add spice to life. Different perspectives bring fresh ideas, creativity and innovation. Without differences, an organization is composed of mere "yes-men." An organization without differences is like a superhighway crossing a flat plain: smooth and boring. An organization that welcomes differences is like a road that twists through a mountain range: difficult to traverse, but exhilirating and varied.

MAINTAINING GOOD WORKING RELATIONSHIPS

Yes, differences are valuable and appealing, but they are accompanied by difficulties. From this perspective, difficult people are more challenging than people like ourselves, but that challenge is worth tackling. The key to dealing with difficult people, therefore, lies in developing good working relationships with people who are different.

How is this done? Harvard professors Roger Fisher and Scott Brown[1] provide several suggestions, which are discussed in the following paragraphs.

Separate Relationship Issues From Substantive Issues

When people at work disagree, two outcomes are in doubt: (1) what decision will be reached and (2) how the individuals will feel about working together in the future. The first question involves the *substantive* issue, how the *content* of the dispute will be resolved. The second involves the relationship issue, how the individuals will deal with each other as people.

You can win at one level and lose at the other—get what you want substantively, yet make an enemy. Or vice-versa—you may not obtain what you want substantively, yet strengthen a working relationship.

To disentangle the two issues, explicitly separate your working relationship with the other person from whether you agree with or approve of his or her viewpoint. That means thinking, "I will treat this person well whether or not I like what he or she thinks or does."

The United States maintains embassies and communicates regularly with officials in the Soviet Union, Afghanistan and Nicaragua—despite disapproving of these countries' policies. If someone at work seems difficult, you might say to yourself:

> *I can and will maintain a decent working relationship with that person, although I don't like what that person does. Our relationship doesn't imply any agreement or approval on my part of that person's behavior. Like governments all over the world, I can keep open*

*lines of communication with people I regard as
difficult or even as enemies. That's the only
way improvement can ever occur. It's possible
and sensible to disentangle substantive and
relationship issues.*

Be Unconditionally Constructive

Many people deal with difficult people in the same way those
people treat them: by reciprocating what they receive. This
may be called an "eye for an eye" policy. If the other person
yells at them, they yell back. If the other person snubs them,
they ignore the other person. If the other person insults them,
they insult that person right back. If the other person cheats
them, they cheat the other person.

The eye for an eye policy is based on a traditional approach to
justice. Unfortunately, in a modern organization, it is largely
ineffectual, even dangerous. Why? The "victim" often is
damaged as much as the perpetrator. Reciprocation sets off a
.negative spiral.

If A lies to B, and B deceives A, what is A likely to do next?
Tell the truth? Unlikely. A probably will lie again—but more
cleverly this time.

If A threatens B and B counterthreatens A, what is A likely to
do? Capitulate? Hardly. A probably will present a more
severe threat or carry out the original threat.

Reciprocation doesn't resolve anything. It doesn't cue A of
being difficult. It just elicits *more* of the same difficult
behavior, and it converts B to A's style of relating. A negative,
escalating, mutually destructive cycle of difficult behavior is
generated.

What's the alternative? Being *unconditionally constructive*. That is, being committed to forging a good working relationship whether or not the other person reciprocates.

You might think that this is a ridiculous solution. Why should you be considerate and constructive when someone else is simply being difficult? There are several reasons. The most important is that it pays off for *you*. Consider your alternatives:

- If the difficult person is being irrationally angry, are you better off responding angrily or responding reasonably? (If you respond angrily, all you produce is a heated battle. If you respond reasonably, you're less likely to do something rash or foolish.)
- If the difficult person won't listen to you, are you better off ignoring that person or trying to understand him or her? (The more you listen to and know about that person, the less you "shoot in the dark" for a solution and the more effectively you deal with the person.)
- If the difficult person breaks a promise to you, are you better off breaking your own promises or keeping your word?
  (If you keep your word, you remain trustworthy and your words will have more impact.)

A good friend of the black educator Booker T. Washington tells of a time they were walking down a city street together. A passerby recognized Dr. Washington. The man's face turned mean, and he deliberately bumped into Washington, uttering a racial slur as he did.

The friend was livid. He asked Dr. Washington, "Aren't you going to retaliate? Give him a tongue lashing!"

Washington smiled patiently and replied, "No. I refuse to let any man cause me to hate."
Washington was determined not to let someone else's behavior, especially a bigot's, determine his own. He insisted on remaining in charge of his own thoughts and behavior, on not following the eye for an eye policy. He chose to be unconditionally constructive.

Beware of Partisan Perceptions
Each of us sees the events of our lives and other peoples' behavior from our own vantage points. Thus, we see only "part" of the whole. We tend to think, nevertheless, that our perspective is accurate and representative of what's occurring.

Unfortunately there are at least two sides to every story and many ways to view every incident. At the end of a hard week, for example, a boss and a subordinate reflect on life in their organization. Each sees things a little differently.

The employee laments, "There's too much paperwork in this organization." The boss complains, "People are always late with their monthly reports."

The employee thinks, "If I were boss, I'd have some control over my life." The boss thinks, "My subordinates have no idea how much pressure I'm under."

The employee feels, "My boss doesn't trust me; he's always looking over my shoulder." The boss feels, "I'm breaking my back to spend time with my people and train them."

The employee thinks, "My boss doesn't appreciate what I do."
The boss thinks, "My employees don't appreciate what I do."

Where you stand on an issue depends, therefore, on where you
sit. In other words, how you think about people depends on
your position. When we judge difficult people, we often forget
that our perceptions of them are only partial. Yet we defend, or
become "partisans," of that perception.

There's much that people do that we don't see. There are
interpretations of our own behavior that we don't consider. A
company president once took a visitor on a tour of corporate
headquarters. On the grounds was a fish pond that the
president said he used to screen job candidates.

The visitor asked, "How?"

"I ask them to look in the fishpond and tell me what they see,"
the president replied. "If they see fish, I hire them. If they see
only their own reflection, I don't."

The company president knows that people who are entranced
with themselves and their partisan perceptions become poor
managers. Those who see other people and understand their
viewpoints are more effective.

Balance Reason With Emotion
We all know that in some instances too much emotion can
diminish performance. The person who is very agitated when
taking a test or giving a speech performs poorly. A person who
becomes furious at a child who commits a minor transgression
hurts rather than helps the child. A person who fears going to
the dentist feels the pain from a toothache escalate.

On the other hand, an organization with little or no emotion is dull and lifeless. Some experts tell us that the most effective leaders are extremely emotional—and even act as cheerleaders—about the goals they're trying to achieve. Parents who coolly lecture their children and rarely hug them or show emotion are doing them a disservice. An appropriate amount of emotion helps a speaker be energetic and vital.

But responding impulsively and emotionally to a difficult person usually only worsens the relationship, especially if the person is making you angry. A good working relationship with a difficult person requires a reasonable approach. What can you do to balance emotional and rational reactions to behavior that upsets you? Fisher and Brown[2] have several suggestions:

Take a break. Ask for a short recess. Go for a walk, get a drink or otherwise interrupt your build-up of emotion. You might even ask to adjourn your meeting and arrange to reconvene on another day.

Count to 10 if an official break isn't possible. That disrupts your upward emotional spiral and gives you a chance to rethink the situation.

Consult a third party. If you feel heated about your relationship with someone, ask for a reaction from a neutral party. You could be overlooking a partisan perception.

Consider the following anecdote. A client once told his lawyer about some litigation he was considering. He asked the lawyer, "How would that case stand up in court?" The lawyer smiled and responded, "No problem. You're sure to win." The client thanked him and started to leave. The lawyer said, "Wait, don't you want me to pursue the case for you?" The client replied, "Nope. What I just told you was the *other guy's* side of the story."

Acknowledge and talk about your emotions. Say, "Excuse me, but this is beginning to make me angry." Or explain precisely what is upsetting you:

"This is frustrating me. When I tried to explain my plan for this account, I was interrupted in midsentence. When I tried to be constructive and suggest that we bring in a consultant, your response—if I recall correctly—was 'Can't you handle this yourself?' What's going on?"

Accept responsibility and apologize if an argument erupts. Say: "I regret that we're having this misunderstanding, and I'm sorry for my part in it. If I have misinterpreted what you were saying or done anything to upset you, I apologize." Such a statement makes it easy for the other person also to accept a portion of the responsibility and to agree to move on to a more reasonable approach. It is mature and constructive, not weak or passive, to accept responsibility for an argument in which you were involved rather than resort to blaming.

Prepare yourself when you know an emotional situation is likely. When a lawyer knows a client will be cross-examined about a stressful event, the lawyer alerts the client beforehand so that the client is braced and ready, rather than surprised and upset, in the witness stand. Likewise, you might think about how you want to act in an upcoming encounter with a difficult person and actively elicit the appropriate emotions within yourself.

Say you're worried that you might feel critical and angry with a difficult person. You'd prefer to be open-minded and optimistic. You can "recruit" the latter feelings by picturing in your mind how you'd like to act—mentally rehearsing the attitude you want to have. You also can dress, stand and practice statements that are consistent with your preferred attitudes. With those rehearsed thoughts fresh in your mind, you're more likely to feel and come across as cool, calm and reasonable in the stressful situation.

Inquire, Listen and Understand

Every year in this country, thousands of companies merge with or are acquired by other companies. A shockingly high percentage of these mergers fall far short of their financial goals. The predominant reason is that people in the acquiring company don't really understand the people, the processes or the culture of its new partner. We can't deal effectively with difficult people unless we understand them. However people usually overestimate their understanding of others.

When you feel that someone is being difficult, it's always best to assume there's a good reason for their behavior that you don't as yet understand. In an interview with *Psychology Today*, psychologist George Miller said, "In order to understand what another person is saying, you must assume that it is true, and try to imagine what it's true of."[3] Unfortunately, most people assume that what other people say is absurd or untrue and try to imagine what could be wrong with them to make them say anything so ridiculous.

The Japanese have an apt story that illustrates how important it is to be open to inquiry, listening and understanding. An American tourist visited a Zen monastery and asked the abbot to explain Zen philosophy to him. The abbot could tell from the American's manner that he already thought Zen to be merely a quaint, archaic, bizarre way of life, so he asked the

---

visitor to join him for a cup of tea. The American was annoyed at this delay, but agreed nonetheless. The abbot set out two cups. He poured tea into the American's cup until it was full, and then continued pouring. The American shouted, "Stop, you can't fit any more tea in there—it's just spilling over the side!" The abbot smiled and replied, "Ah, and that's what would happen if I tried to explain Zen to you. Your mind is already full of preconceptions. You have no space to receive what I would say. My words would simply pour over the sides. Empty your mind. Become open to learning, and then we can speak meaningfully."

In the same way, we must first empty our minds of preconceptions about difficult people. We must not assume we understand them. We must ask ourselves, "What do they care about?" Studies by Harvard psychologist David McClelland, for example, indicate that people are primarily motivated by one of three things: (1) *achievement* (the desire to do interesting work and do it well), (2) *affiliation* (the desire to form good relationships with people) or (3) *power* (the desire to achieve status and influence). Many people who are motivated by achievement think affiliation-oriented people are lazy socialites and power-oriented people are do-nothing bureaucrats. People motivated by affiliation might think achievement-oriented people are workaholics and power-oriented people are heartless. People who want power may view the other two types of people as spinning their wheels and getting nowhere. People who jump to these types of conclusions forget that other people may have different interests and desires—march to a different drummer—than they do.

A student once asked a professor to teach him the secret to the art of conversation. The professor said he'd be glad to. The student waited. The professor remained silent. The student finally blurted out, "I'm listening." The professor replied, "Aha, now you know!"

Consult Before Deciding

When people work closely together, what one person does usually affects the others. (This interdependence certainly applies to members of a family.) Yet we often make decisions or take actions that affect other people without consulting them or even notifying them in advance. Doing so, unfortunately, usually upsets the people who are kept in the dark and destroys good working relationships.

Why do we sometimes neglect to consult those affected by our actions? Usually, it simply doesn't occur to us, or we assume there's no need for it. Perhaps we think we already know what the other person will say. Or we're sure we've made the right decision and feel we have the authority to make it. So we just "tell" the other person what we've done and expect that person to accept it.

But people don't like being controlled by others, even if what's decided is substantively in their own best interests. People like to participate in decision-making, even if they would have made the same decision anyway. So it's best always to consult anyone who will be affected by any of your decisions. This doesn't mean giving up your right to decide.

Consulting merely involves letting someone know that you are considering and soliciting input about a particular matter and that you are taking that input seriously. When you consult others before making a decision, they feel as if you see them as important, as a meaningful player in the decision-making process. When people don't feel coerced into accepting a decision, they are more understanding and accepting of the decision. Consulting others before deciding leads to being appreciated rather than to being viewed as a difficult person.

Be Trustworthy

Working relationships are better among trustworthy people. People who can be counted on to keep their word are trustworthy. Trustworthiness is not an objective measure of honesty and reliability. It is a qualitative measure. If I *believe* you will do what you say, then I perceive you as trustworthy. If I suspect you won't, your credibility with me is low.

Faith in people is fragile. Once broken, it's hard to restore. You may think: "I have good intentions; I usually come through with most things I promise; I'm not trying to hurt anyone; I should be trusted." But being trustworthy in three out of five instances doesn't earn you trust. Every single breach of trust diminishes people's confidence in you. Even if you keep your word nine out of 10 times, others will remember the one time you didn't and wonder when you will disappoint them next. (Many people's trust is as disproportional as the man who told the dictionary author, "You're disgusting. I've read your book and there are at least 10 instances of profanity in it!")

Sometimes we make promises carelessly—when we say, for example, "I'll be home by 6:00" without checking our calendars. Or we treat promises lightly, saying "Don't worry, I'll take care of that" to reassure someone and then neglect to follow up in the press of other events. Sometimes we tell little white lies, such as "I never got the message" or "I tried to reach you" to someone we should have called back. These apparently insignificant breaches of trust gradually erode our

---

credibility and encourage others to indulge in their now "difficult" behavior.

Most people believe themselves to be more trustworthy than others think they are. We forgive ourselves more readily for minor transgressions that linger in other peoples' minds. *We* know why we neglected to do something. *We* know we had a good reason and intended no harm. But others can't read our minds or know what our lives are like. All they know is they've been let down. And to them we're "difficult" people.

We can improve our trustworthiness by taking our promises seriously and making an effort to fulfill them—by being on time for appointments, for example. Also, when we know ahead of time, we can warn people about obstacles that are likely to interfere with our keeping commitments. We also can honestly admit, explain, apologize and offer to do whatever it takes to compensate for our broken commitments when they do occur.

We can help other people be more trustworthy as well. We shouldn't tempt people too much, "overloading" them with trust. If someone leaves money lying around and people take it, who is at fault? No just the thief. The person negligent with the funds is guilty of "trust overloading." Most firms hire auditors to go over their books, not because the firms suspect their employees of stealing, but because that precaution keeps opportunities for violating trust to a minimum.

Society abounds with examples of "trust control." Banks seek collateral on loans, landlords collect security deposits when renting apartments and customs inspectors examine the luggage of overseas travelers. All do so to keep trust within manageable bounds. Likewise, you can help unreliable employees be more trustworthy by incorporating more "auditing procedures" into their work—by more frequently checking their progress and performance.

Be wary, though, of "underloading" people with trust. Peering over peoples' shoulders in perpetual distrust damages their trustworthiness. Backseat drivers don't help youngsters develop their own driving judgment. If I frequently suspect you of unreliable behavior, I eventually create a self-fulfilling prophecy—you begin to think dishonesty is normal and expected. To avoid trust underloading, many businesses have employees perform their own quality inspections rather than use quality inspectors. Separating production from quality control had created, in many cases, a division between the two functions. Producers thought "What can I get away with?" and inspectors thought "What can I catch?" If you assume people don't care about their work, soon they won't.

When untrustworthy behavior occurs, we must control our anger. Perhaps we're overreacting based on our own perceptions and biases. What you may view as intentional betrayal may be mere forgetfulness or misinterpretation of expectations. Or you may be giving your own needs higher priority than the other person does. (A mother once was asked how her children's marriages were going. She replied, "My daughter married a wonderful man. He buys her expensive gifts, takes her on lavish vacations and brings her breakfast in bed. My son married a terribly selfish woman. She expects expensive gifts, lavish vacations and breakfast in bed!")

Treat disappointing or difficult behavior as a *joint problem*, not as a crime. When someone doesn't do what you expect, don't simply accuse or blame. Ask "What can *we* do to be sure this doesn't occur again?"

Use Persuasion, not Coercion

When people are being difficult and you have more authority than they do, it's tempting to *force* or *coerce* them to do as you wish. But compliance through coercion—such as threatening harm—provides only short-term gains and long-term losses. People resent being coerced and eventually express that resentment in angry outbursts or acts of revenge. Coercion creates competition to see who will "win," and methods to create win/win solutions are overlooked. Rather than resolve difficulties, coercion usually just perpetuates or escalates them.

A difficulty should be seen as a problem that both parties wish to solve through cooperation. Both should be on the "same side of the line," attacking the problem, not each other. Managing difficult behavior is not a contest; it's a challenge to invent a solution both people support and feel committed to implementing.

To do this, neither party can afford to adhere to only one way of handling the problem. An either/or, "take it or leave it," approach usually creates a standoff or results in one party coercing the other or giving up in despair.

Remember the story of the two frogs thrown into the center of a huge vat of milk. One looked around, couldn't see the rim, gave up on survival, sank to the bottom and drowned. The other, thinking there had to be a way out of the predicament, kept swimming. By morning he was standing safely atop a pile of butter his churning had created.

If people continue thinking, talking and attempting to persuade each other of what's best, the law of requisite variety will begin to apply. That law, paraphrased from the world of cybernetics, states that the person who has one more alternative than the number of obstacles he or she faces eventually will triumph. In other words, "where there's a will (and available alternatives), there'll be a way."

Accept and Deal Seriously With Difficult People

It's tempting to scorn and reject people who don't fulfill our expectations. When disappointed, we become critical and disdainful. We slam the door on communication and give up on problem solving.

But we have to remember that the action that upsets us is only a small part of the difficult person's constellation of behavior. Consider, for example, the advertising executive who mishandled an account and had to report it to his board of directors. He started his talk by posting in front of the room a large sheet of white paper with a small black dot on it. He asked the board members to tell him what they saw. They said, naturally, "A small black dot."

The executive said, "Yes, and there's also a large white sheet of paper. Notice that when something is blemished, we attend to that small blemish and overlook the broad background on which it is placed. I hope you'll keep that background in mind when I make my report this morning."

The difficult behavior of many people is simply a small dot on a large background. Be sure to keep that background in mind. Let the offending person know you are aware of his or her positive qualities. Even if the person is a support worker, he or she is equally a human being and worthy of basic respect. Treating people with acceptance and respect, even if their behavior is difficult at times, provides the groundwork for improvements.

✍ EXERCISE 5: Preventing Difficulties

Review the prevention strategies discussed in this chapter and complete the following sentence:

To better prevent difficulties with my co-workers and to build good working relationships with them, I will increase

_____

_____

_____

_____

_____

_____

******

ENDNOTES

1. Roger Fisher and Scott Brown, *Getting Together: Building a Relationship That Gets to Yes* (Boston: Houghton-Mifflin, 1988).

2. Ibid., 53-59.

3. George A. Miller, "Giving Away Psychology in the 80's," *Psychology Today* (January 1980): 38.

HOW TO DEAL WITH DIFFICULT PEOPLE

BEING THE SOLUTION, NOT THE PROBLEM

When two people don't get along, each usually blames the other for the problem:

> "He started it!"
>
> "I'm doing the best I can."
>
> "What else can I do when she acts that way?"

Have you ever had these or similar thoughts? Most people have. When self-justifying thoughts are running through your mind, what do you suppose other people are thinking?

The same thing, of course!

They assume you're the cause. You assume they're the cause. And the war goes on.

You each believe things would be better if only *the other person* would change. You certainly can *try* to change difficult people. But think about your own past experience: Have you ever found it easy to change someone? Probably not. People resist being changed.

THE IMPORTANCE OF CHANGING *YOU*

Unless people are willing to change, change is unlikely. You can't reach into their minds and change how they think. In truth, the person you can control most readily is *yourself*. You have direct access only to your *own* thoughts, body and speech.

When you change, other people also are likely to change voluntarily. Why? People behave differently in different situations. So when you change your behavior, others naturally adapt themselves to your new behavior.

Don't you communicate differently with each of these people: your boss, support workers, best friend, worst enemy, small child, frail elderly person, doctor, door-to-door salesperson, police officer, panhandler and so on. The common denominator in all your communication situations is you. Yet your behavior differs somewhat depending on the individual with whom you are communicating. What variable alters your behavior? Primarily, it's how the other person treats you!

So, if you treat difficult people differently, they will respond differently—and probably not be so difficult any more. Keep in mind that the difficult people you encounter usually think you're the one who's being difficult. When asked to explain their difficult behavior, they'll usually say it's in response to you. So, if you change, other people no longer believe they have reason to be difficult.

You may still be thinking that you know some truly difficult people—they're simply difficult individuals and what you do is irrelevant. Perhaps that's so. But, unfortunately, many people inadvertantly "trigger" other people's difficult behaviors that bother them most.

Here are a few examples:

Max has been reserved in the group for several meetings. When he finally speaks, he feels hurt when the others don't pay much attention to his suggestions. (Who's the "difficult" party, quiet Max or the impervious group members?)

Jackie is overburdened with work, yet she almost invariably says "yes" when her colleagues request her assistance. (Who's really difficult, agreeable Jackie or her demanding co-workers?)

Ted is authoritative and patronizing with the women who work for him. He's suddenly shocked to learn that sweet, petite Linda has been quietly manipulating him into making a fool of himself. (Who's more difficult, macho Ted or manipulative Linda?)

SAGS AND SAPS

All three of these individuals probably feel they're dealing with difficult people. Actually, they're engaging in self-defeating behavior—they're eliciting from other people the behaviors they find difficult to handle. Donald Bowen of the University of Tulsa calls these communication patterns *Self-Annihilating Games*, or SAGs for short.[1] And he calls SAG perpetrators SAPs, for *Self-Annihilating Person*.

A SAG is a repetitive, self-maintaining, unsatisfying pattern of communicating in which at least one party, the SAP, is both the initiator and the victim.

Everyone practices a SAG or two. They're frustrating, but normal—not an indicator of a character flaw or mental illness.

A SAP needs *collaborators*—and these collaborators often are characterized as "difficult" people. Sometimes these collaborators clearly behave unpleasantly—for example, they may yell, but only after the SAP has yelled at them.

Sometimes the SAP only imagines the collaborator's behavior—a salesperson may not make a call because he *imagines* a customer will slam the door in his face.

Here's the usual SAG sequence:

1. The SAP has a negative image of him or herself or other people and behaves in a way reflecting that image, starting the SAG.
2. The collaborator(s) perceives that behavior and reacts "logically," given the SAP's behavior.
3. The SAP perceives the collaborator's actions, labels them "difficult," strengthens his or her original negative image and intensifies the SAG behavior.

Here's an example. In his book *Working*, Studs Terkel reports the comments of Larry Ross, a retired executive who views the business world as a jungle. Ross says: "The executive is a lonely animal in the jungle who doesn't have a friend. ... Deep down, they're scared stiff. The fear is there. You can smell it. You can see it in their faces. I'm not so sure you couldn't see it on my face many, many times during my climb up."

Ross starts the SAG sequence, then, with the belief that people in business are aggressive predators, and it's scary to him. Ross continues, "You're always on guard. Did you ever see a jungle animal that wasn't on guard?" And he is contemptuous of trust, "The most stupid phrase anyone can use in business is loyalty." Believing the best defense is a good offense, he manages his support workers by fear: "I always said, 'If you do a good job, I'll give you a great reward. You'll keep your job.'"

If Ross sees all his support workers as disloyal, self-seeking, untrustworthy jungle animals waiting to pounce on him if he makes the slightest slip, it's understandable that he views himself as unsafe and untrusted and reinforces this image in every interaction with his support workers.

Let's trace Ross's thinking in our three-step model:

1. He thinks: "Everyone's out to get me. I'm in constant danger." His behavior is hostile and distrusting.
2. His employees see him as hostile, dangerous, threatening and exploitive. So they react "logically" by protecting themselves, withholding information, telling him only what he wants to hear and undermining him when they can.
3. Ross perceives their behavior, feels confirmed in his belief that they're difficult and dangerous people and escalates his own manipulative management style.

Ross created the difficult people who worked for him.

Do you recognize yourself or people you know in the following SAGs?

SAG #1: The Wallflower
SAP's Self-Perception: "I don't have any ideas or experiences others will find interesting."

SAP's Behavior: is very quiet and reserved; hangs back during meetings and social occasions

Collaborator's Perception: "Wallflower doesn't have much to say."

Collaborator's Logical Reaction: ignores Wallflower; interrupts or tunes out Wallflower

SAP's Perception of Collaborator's Difficult Behavior: "What a cold, uncaring, aloof person. Obviously someone not interested in me."

SAG #2: The Scaredy-Cat
SAP's Self-Perception: "If I speak frankly and openly about myself, I might look foolish and be vulnerable."

SAP's Behavior: makes only small talk and doesn't bring up anything personal or important

Collaborator's Perception: "Cat seems superficial, closed, distant and uncomfortable talking about feelings."

Collaborator's Logical Reaction: When Cat's around, make small talk. Don't raise topics likely to make Cat uncomfortable.

SAP's Perception of Collaborator's Difficult Behavior: "These people are uptight. They speak on the surface and seem unwilling to become personal friends. They're probably cold fishes, purely out for themselves."

SAG #3: The Pollyanna
SAP's Self-Perception: "If I say anything negative, peoples' feelings will be hurt, and they'll become upset."

SAP's Behavior: shares only positive feelings; is always polite, formal and courteous

Collaborator's Perception: "Pollyanna doesn't seem strong enough to deal with strong feelings or negative reactions."

Collaborator's Logical Reaction: Avoid confronting Pollyanna or bringing up anything unpleasant.

SAP's Perception of Collaborator's Difficult Behavior: "I was right. They can't deal with reality. They never say what they really think."

SAG #4: The Macho Man
SAP's Self-Perception: "If I don't prove I'm a real man, people will think I'm a wimp."

SAP's Behavior: acts super-tough; super-masculine

Collaborator's Perception: "M-M is one tough, mean hombre."

Collaborator's Logical Reaction: (Men): I'll compete with him to show I'm as much a man as he is. (Women): Flatter and manipulate M-M.

SAP's Perception of Collaborator's Difficult Behavior: "You've got to be tough in a world where most people are trying to compete with you or manipulate and exploit you— and the rest are wimps."

SAG #5: The "Fluffy"
SAP's Self-Perception: "It's a man's world and a woman needs someone to take care of her."

SAP's Behavior: is passive, self-deprecating, flattering to men, doesn't take women seriously

Collaborator's Perception: (Macho Man): "My kind of woman." (Others): "What a bubblehead."

Collaborator's Logical Reaction: Macho Man pursues her. Others distrust, discount or take advantage of her.

SAP's Perception of Collaborator's Difficult Behavior: "I'd better stick close to Macho Man or these other people will run right over me."

SAG #6: The Underdog
SAP's Self-Perception: "I feel powerless and that frightens me."

SAP's Behavior: does whatever people in power want (dependent) or does only what people in power don't want (counter-dependent)

Collaborator's Perception: (of Dependent Underdog): "What a yes-man." (of Counterdependent Underdog): "What a nut."

Collaborator's Logical Reaction: ignore or take advantage of Dependent Underdog; avoid or attack Counterdependent Underdog

SAP's Perception of Collaborator's Difficult Behavior: "It just goes to show how little power I have around here."

SAG #7: The Egotist
SAP's Self-Perception: "People are fascinated by me, and they aren't very effective if I don't help them."

SAP's Behavior: boastful, self-centered, domineering

Collaborator's Perception: "What a fathead. I'd better just go along—he or she never listens."

Collaborator's Logical Reaction: listen politely; tolerate Egotist's delusions

SAP's Perception of Collaborator's Difficult Behavior: "They worship me. They wouldn't know what to do without me."

SAG #8: The Old Softy
SAP's Self-Perception: "If I'm really nice to people, they'll love and appreciate me."

SAP's Behavior: Unable to say "no"; disorganized and overworked; can't prioritize because he or she doesn't accept validity of own needs

Collaborator's Perception: "Old Softy's awfully nice, but not very effective."

Collaborator's Logical Reaction: takes advantage of Softy by overloading with unimportant tasks, but avoids giving important assignments or promotion to key positions

SAP's Perception of Collaborator's Difficult Behavior: "See, they do appreciate me. They keep giving me more to do."

SAG #9: Mr. Spock
SAP's Self-Perception: "If we start expressing feelings, I could lose control of myself and the situation."

SAP's Behavior: Emphasizes rationality; avoids "emotions"

Collaborator's Perception: "Spock doesn't care how I feel."

Collaborator's Logical Reaction: deal with Spock only in rational, businesslike terms; suppress emotions of excitment, irritation, fear, warmth and so forth

SAP's Perception of Collaborator's Difficult Behavior: "I need to increase my control of this situation because these people don't have their hearts into it."

SAG #10: The Perfectionist
SAP's Self-Perception: "If my work isn't perfect, I'll appear mediocre or foolish."

SAP's Behavior: compulsive perfectionism; avoids errors at any cost; overworked and overstressed

Collaborator's Perception: "I sure don't want to work for Perfectionist," or "Perfectionist gets things done right no matter what."

Collaborator's Logical Reaction: avoids being evaluated or controlled by perfectionist or assigns toughest jobs to Perfectionist

SAP's Perception of Colaborator's Difficult Behavior: "They give me all the tough, dirty jobs to do, but not enough help to get them done."

✍️ Exercise 6: Self-Annihilating Games

Review the 10 SAG examples in this chapter. Do you find yourself in any?

If you do, relate that SAG to the "difficult" behavior you identified in Exercise 2. Do you somehow generate the behavior you dislike? If so, what change in your own behavior is likely to reduce the difficult behavior of the other person?

_____

_____

_____

_____

******

OVERCOMING SAGs

How can SAGs be overcome? Consider the following factors:

Awareness. Just being aware that you might play a role in someone else's difficult behavior helps you be alert for the SAG and minimize its occurence.

Feedback. SAPs who aren't aware they are triggering a SAG need to be told that they are doing so. Even after people recognize their roles in an ongoing SAG, they may not be aware of the behavior that set the SAG in motion and, therefore, continue to exhibit the behavior. Such people may need feedback—a warning or a "yellow caution light"—from another person involved or from an onlooker.

Support. Because changing a customary way of dealing with people can be unsettling, the SAP may need support. But the type of support needed may vary from person to person. Some people prefer a tough-minded scolding each time they return to their old ways. Others prefer gentle reminders and encouragement. The person changing should identify which type of support he or she considers more helpful.

Alternative Behaviors. Sometimes a SAG continues because the SAP simply doesn't know any other way to handle the situation. Bowen gives this example, a variation on the "Old Softy" SAG.[3] Sue, a bright and conscientious woman, was personnel manager for a chain of fast-food restaurants. Her "difficult" people were the other managers (all male) who ate lunch together. When they left for a restaurant, rather than invite Sue along, they would ask her to listen for any important phone calls they were expecting. Sue wanted to be invited to lunch, but she felt that asking would be "too pushy."

Bowen asked Sue to do a "role-reversal," to imagine she was in her male colleagues' shoes. He played her part and said, "It bothers me that you guys leave me to watch the phones while you go to lunch. The secretaries could easily handle all incoming calls, and I'd like to participate in your discussions of how we run this place." Sue felt that approach was reasonable. She now had an alternative to her situation. She tried it, and was readily included in the lunch group. Sue managed the difficult people at her job by frankly revealing her own thoughts about the situation.

A recent study of executive self-development indicates that SAGs present crucial challenges for moving ahead in organizations.[4] Researchers interviewed 22 executives and found these common barriers to their career growth:

- the power of the position makes others afraid to give them feedback
- their orientation to action discourages introspection
- their need to appear competent makes it difficult for them to accept criticism
- their history of success makes it difficult for them to recognize the need to change when old ways are no longer appropriate

These findings indicate that managers, especially, need to ask themselves this question: "Am I doing something to *create* the difficulty I'm facing." Questioning your own behavior can be one of your best defenses against difficult people.

ENDNOTES

1. Donald Bowen, "Self-Annihilating Games in Interpersonal Relations," *Journal of Teaching Behavior* 10(3): 31-44.

2. Studs Terkel, *Working: People Talk About What They Do All Day and How They Feel About What They Do* (New York: Pantheon, 1974): 405-413.

3. Bowen.

4. R.E. Kaplan, W.H. Drath, and J.R. Kofomides, *High Hurdles: The Challenge of Executive Self-Development* (Tech. Rep. No. 25, Greensboro, SC: Center for Creative Leadership, 1985).

DIFFICULT MODES OF TALK

It is easy to deal with someone who wants what we do and does what we want. We usually consider people "difficult" only when we disagree with them. But conflict isn't always unpleasant. You probably know several people who act and think differently than you do, but you like and respect them anyway.

Why, then, do we experience some people as difficult when we conflict with them? The explanation lies in how they *express* their different viewpoints. Certain modes of expressing an opinion are especially annoying. They evoke negative emotions in listeners, and those emotions give rise to hostile responses that exacerbate the conflict.

MODES OF COMMUNICATION

Psychologist Virginia Satir[1] identifies five ways people air their opinions when disagreement exists. The more people are under stress, the more consistently they employ their customary mode of self-expression. See if you can identify which mode is most characteristic of the difficult people you know:

Blaming
People who use the Blamer mode assume they are right and you are wrong; they are innocent and you are guilty; they are good and you are bad. They exaggerate what's going on by using words like: "every," "always," "never," "nobody," and

"nothing" to make accusations or threats. They give orders.
Their body language is threatening. They shake their fingers or
bang the table. They frown and scowl. They speak loudly or
talk through their teeth like Clint Eastwood. They also stress
key words very strongly, as in "You simply don't CONsider
what ANYbody else in the firm might want. You ALways do
things YOUR way!"

Placating
People using the Placater mode are overly eager to avoid
offending anyone. They praise excessively ("How wonderful!"
or "That's really great!"). They plead and cajole. They hedge
even the smallest request heavily ("If it wouldn't be too much
trouble . . ."). Their body language is like that of a cocker
spaniel puppy—wide-eyed, smiling and affectionate. They use
"I/you" words a lot and are vocally expressive. A typical
Placating utterance is "Sure, SURE, whatever YOU'D like is
perfectly FINE with ME!"

Computing
People in the Computer mode use generalizations and abstrac-
tions rather than personal references ("Generally, what's done
is . . ." or "The bottom line here is . . ."). They try to relay
emotionless, neutral messages ("The fact of the matter is . . ."
rather than "I feel . . ."). They use minimal body language:
they're poker-faced, have a flat tone of voice and gesture very
little. A typical Computer utterance is: "Let's not react
emotionally. Let's understand the basic principles and
establish precise standard operating procedures here."

Distracting
People in a Distractor mode don't want to face the
disagreement directly, so they skip from one approach to
another ("This makes sense . . . On the other hand . . . Oh, who

knows?") They may joke about the conflict or talk at length about minor, tangential issues—apparently forgetting the major issue that's still unresolved. Often they seem disorganized, even panicked, as if they don't know how they want to proceed. Sometimes they cycle between several of the other modes, at first Blaming, then Placating, then Computing. A typical Distracting utterance might be: "I can't believe you did this! But I'm sure you had a good reason. Oh, Lord, what'll we do now? Let's figure this out. I'll never forget the time this happened at my other firm . . ."

Leveling

Leveling is telling the truth about what you perceive, think, or feel to the best extent possible. It calls for facing a situation as directly and as personally as you can. The Leveler breaks through facades to get at what's really happening and why. Leveling may involve revealing the hidden agenda ("What I really think about this issue . . ." or "To be very frank, it seems to me . . ."). Leveler utterances vary a great deal. In fact, Leveling is characterized best by the *absence* of the other modes—there's no faultfinding, fault-avoiding or evasion of the feelings or real issues involved.

✍ Exercise 7: Communication Modes

When you talk with the difficult person you identified in Exercise 1, which of these five communication modes does that person use most often? _____

Which do you use? _____

******

RESPONSE STRATEGIES

Suzette Haden Elgin suggests several strategies for responding to difficult people who frequently use one of these communication modes.[2]

Like Begets Like

The first is based on the principle that *anything you feed will grow*. Communication is a feedback loop. In other words, like begets like. If you respond in the same mode as the difficult person or *match* the other person's approach, here's what will happen:

- Blaming someone who is blaming you will create a confrontation.
- Placating someone who is placating you creates a wishy-washy "After you. No, after you" two-step and results in an undignified delay.
- Computing with someone who is computing also creates a two-step, except the delay appears far more dignified and significant.
- Distracting when someone else also is distracting builds avoidance on top of avoidance, creating a growing sense of panic.
- Leveling with someone who is leveling with you— sending the simple truth both ways—generally leads to greater mutual understanding, compromise and new ideas for solving the problem.

So, your first decision is whether the mode being used by the difficult person is something you want to encourage. If it is, match that mode. Otherwise, choose another mode for responding.

When in Doubt, Be a Computer

When you don't know which mode to choose, maintain the Computer mode until you have enough information to make a reasoned choice. Doing so will draw the other person into that mode, which generally is innocuous and safe.

Why?

Many times people are triggered into their habitual mode because they feel extreme stress. They are upset and not consciously aware of what they are doing. As a reflex, they automatically start blaming, placating, distracting or disclosing. And they'll do this consistently when they feel scared.

What do they fear?

- When people feel helpless or powerless, they snap into the Blamer mode to regain their loss of control.
- When people fear others will be angry and reject them, they snap into the Placater mode to regain their approval.
- When people feel alarmed by the intensity of their own or others' emotions, they snap into the Computer mode in an attempt to bury those emotions.
- When people have no idea how they feel about a situation, they snap into the Distractor mode to avoid taking a stand of any kind.
- When people cannot tolerate the vagueness or phoniness of a situation, they snap into the Leveling mode to bring real feelings and issues out in the open.

You should maintain the Computer mode just long enough to gather your thoughts and assess the situation. Shifting temporarily into that mode allows you to avoid impulsively making an inappropriate move and provides a momentary respite while you consciously decide on your preferred mode.

Implement Your Preferred Mode

When you sense which mode is most appropriate for the situation at hand, you can strategically choose and implement it. How do you decide which mode is best?

First you need to know, as certainly as you can, the mode of the other person. If, for example, someone says, "I'll go along with whatever you suggest," you should take a moment to assess whether the person is in a Placater or a Leveler mode. If in a Placater mode, the person is temporarily trying to regain your good graces—not genuinely empty of opinions and ready to go along with what you propose. Once the person no longer fears upsetting you, he or she is likely to voice a preference, be annoyed with the decision you made and subtly sabotage it.

If in a Leveler mode, however, the person's willingness to support your proposal is genuine and you can advocate and implement your idea.

How can you tell which mode you're facing? Elgin suggests: "Watch for mismatch. The clash between the words and the body language of the speaker, as well as the way the intonation differs from normal stress patterns, will always give you the necessary clues."[3]

For most people, up to 90 percent of emotional information is expressed through nonverbal cues when speaking. And the most revealing aspect of nonverbal communication is the voice: its quality, tone and intonation.

You already have stored in your mind tacit knowledge of the nonverbal cues that indicate a person's mode. Let's examine again the example of differentiating Leveling from Placating messages. Test your ability to make this distinction in the following way: Imagine you're going out for the evening with someone whose tastes in entertainment differ dramatically from yours (he loves horror films, you prefer comedies; she likes steak, you're a vegetarian). Next, imagine you want this person's approval very much, and you fear the evening will be ruined unless you go along with what he or she wants. Down deep you resent this selfishness, but for the time being you're willing to indulge it in order to make the evening work. From this Placater frame of mind say aloud, "I'll go along with whatever you suggest."

Next, imagine it's another occasion—you're about to go out with a friend (also with dissimilar tastes) who will be entering the hospital the next day for a life-threatening operation. You genuinely want this evening to be delightful for your partner and you want to indulge his or her every whim. From this Leveling frame of mind say again, "I'll go along with whatever you suggest."

Can you hear the difference in your tone of voice? Did you notice any differences in your posture, facial expression or gestures? You probably had little difficulty detecting the difference between the modes used in those two identical utterances. (You might ask a friend to read the preceding section and repeat the exercise, not telling you which mode is being used first. You'll probably have little difficulty detecting the actual mode.)

Once you know the other person's mode, you can choose your own. Remember the basic principle: anything you feed will grow. So, if you want

- a *delay*, use the computer or distractor mode.
- *to make the decision yourself*, first use the Placater mode—to trigger a Placater response in the other person—and then decide.
- the *other person to decide*, just level and say so.
- *the conversation to be honest*, shift to the Leveling mode yourself.

Knowing about and recognizing communication modes is very helpful when you deal with difficult people. Many systems exist for categorizing individuals into one type of "character" or another. (See the first chapter of this book for a discussion of the system Robert Bramson describes in *Dealing With Difficult People*.) But you as well as others are likely to shift from one communication mode to another depending on the demands of your situation. Managing difficult communication modes is preferable to labeling yourself or another person permanently as a particular type of character. Consider communication modes as different dance steps you can shift into when the music changes. Don't assume you or anyone else dances to the same tune all the time.

ENDNOTES

1. Virginia Satir, *The New Peoplemaking* (Mountain View, CA: Science and Behavior Books, 1988).

2. Suzette Haden Elgin, *Success With the Gentle Art of Verbal Self-Defense*, (Englewood Cliffs, NJ: Prentice-Hall, 1989).

3. Ibid.

ENCOURAGING
DESIRABLE BEHAVIOR

There are two ways to manage difficult people. One is to decrease their difficult behavior. The other is to increase the behavior we approve of. We do the former more often: We notice and criticize shortcomings. We "catch" others doing something wrong. Too often, unfortunately, we take for granted and overlook all there is to appreciate and encourage.

TRACKING POSITIVES

People respond better to praise than to criticism. They are willing to work harder for someone who recognizes and appreciates what they do well than for someone who picks at whatever they do poorly.

But you may think: "People won't change or improve unless their shortcomings are pointed out. Praise only entrenches the status quo."

Not necessarily. One international pharmaceutical company, for example, uses a program called "Tracking Positives" to train its salespeople. Here's how it works.

The instructor explains the selling skills the company wants its salespeople to use. The trainees work in pairs to practice selling the company's products to each other. Observers look for "positives"—desirable behaviors.

Following each practice round, the observers track the positives of each salesperson, pointing out all behaviors they believe will make that salesperson successful. No one mentions any negative or undesirable behaviors.

During each round, trainees have opportunities to practice selling and to track the positives of other trainees. Between rounds, the positives from the preceding rounds are reviewed; trainees are encouraged to maintain them; and an additional skill to practice is identified.

The participants feel appreciated and encouraged. Their self-confidence increases, and they enjoy learning. They learn from observing others' good points. And they avoid the embarrassment and inhibition usually caused by critical feedback. The instructors insist on tracking only positives because they consider it an efficient way to teach.

But you don't have to be teaching in order to track positives. If you comment on what pleases you in other people's behavior, they will enjoy their work more, enjoy being around you and feel more motivated to do things for you. As Blanchard and Johnson say in *The One-Minute Manager,* try to catch people doing something right.[1]

Think of someone you consider "difficult." In Exercise 8, list three very specific things that person did in the last week that you *liked.* (Examples might be: "Told me honestly what he thought," "Apologized when he made a mistake," or "Left me alone to do the job my own way.")

✍ Exercise 8: Tracking Positives

Three desirable behaviors that a person I consider difficult has performed in the last week:

1. _____
   _____
   _____
   _____
   _____
   _____
   _____

2. _____
   _____
   _____
   _____
   _____
   _____
   _____

3. _____
   _____
   _____
   _____
   _____
   _____
   _____

******

CONVEYING PRAISE MESSAGES

Next, let's examine the ways you can convey that a desirable behavior pleases you. Helen Hall Clinard[2] identifies the following nonverbal communication, words and actions that people use to express appreciation:

Nonverbal Communication	Words	Actions
Smiling	Saying "thank you"	Giving a gift
Nodding	Telling someone else about it	Buying a drink
Waving	Requesting that it be done again	Presenting an award
Giving a thumbs up	Saying "good," bravo," "terrific"	Inviting the person to lunch
Clasping and raising hands	Praising the person	Increasing responsibilities
Shaking hands	Giving a message of appreciation	Designating a new job title
Giving a pat on the back		Behaving similarly

These methods of expressing appreciation aren't applicable in all situations. They are merely alternatives for letting someone know that you are aware of a particular behavior and like it.

Now, look back at the list of three "positives" you identified in Exercise 8. Did you let that person know you noticed and liked each one?

If not, which of the ways previously listed could you have used? Which will you use the next time that person does something positive?

Granted, giving praise isn't always easy or even desirable, especially to someone who usually is difficult. Praise sometimes is perceived as insincere, patronizing, false, manipulative or a way of "buttering someone up," breeding complacency or raising false expectations. No wonder people underuse praise!

But if used properly, praise can be effective. What makes the difference between praise that works and praise that backfires?

- *Sincerity.* You must genuinely believe that what you are praising is a "positive." Avoid phony praise!
- *Specificity.* Your praise must be concrete, not vague. "I found your report easy to follow" is much more specific than "Good job on the report." Specific messages are helpful and believable.
- *Disclosure vs. Evaluation.* Praise that describes your personal experience is better than praise that evaluates the other person. (Compare again the two praise messages in the last paragraph.) If you're not an expert on the kind of behavior you're praising, your evaluation may be inaccurate or unappreciated.

Effective praising, therefore, clearly states:

- the specific behavior you like
- how this behavior is helpful
- how you feel as a result of this help

Imagine that you are an employee who stayed late one night to help your boss meet an important deadline.

What's the specific behavior? Staying after hours on Tuesday night to help complete a project.

How was this behavior helpful? The boss was able to meet the deadline.

How does the boss feel? Relieved and grateful.

Imagine that you received this message of praise from your boss:

> "I really appreciate your staying late to help me Tuesday night. I was very relieved to get the project done properly and sent off on time. I couldn't have done either without you."

Would you:

- Know the specific behavior your boss appreciates?
- Know how the behavior was useful to her?
- Know how she felt about it?
- Believe the sincerity of the message?
- Feel more positive about yourself?
- Feel more positive about her?
- Feel motivated to continue or repeat the behavior?

If your answer was "yes" to most or all of these questions, you can see the importance of each element.

✍ Exercise 9: Messages of Praise

Take a minute now to write out an equivalent message of
praise regarding any one of the three "positives" you identified
for your "difficult" person: _____

_____

_____

******

MAKE IT A HABIT

You may think that following the "formula" proposed here is
out of place and awkward in interpersonal relationships. You
may value spontaneity and sincerity in your communication
with people and fear that following this formula would
interfere more than help.

Of course, artificiality kills communication as badly as a
vague, judgmental message might. But keep in mind that
spontaneity is dependent on habits. We spontaneously do
things that are motivated by feelings and flow from habit.

Habits are based on practice. Habitually doing what doesn't
work just gets you deeper into hot water. The period of initial
awkwardness you will experience until you've consciously
used a new behavior frequently enough to make it a habit is a
worthwhile investment of your energy.

Actually, tracking positives with messages of appreciation is a
relatively easy and risk-free way to deal with difficult people.
Although some people may at first view your positive
messages with skepticism, they will soon learn to value your

appreciation if you are sincere, and you gradually will develop a more satisfactory and productive relationship.

THE CONDITIONAL APPRECIATION MESSAGE

Say your difficult person really isn't "out to get you." In fact, the person wants to please you, but he or she isn't doing a good job of it right now.

You might have to wait a long time for the desired behavior to occur (perhaps by accident) before you can affirm it. However, by varying the standard appreciation message slightly, you can encourage the behavior you want *before* it occurs. Simply describe the specific behavior you *would* like, how it *would* help you and how you *would* feel about it. Here are some examples:

> *"Jack, I'd appreciate a week's notice before the next report is needed. That allows me to gather accurate and up-to-date information without feeling rushed. Doing it that way would be much more pleasant for me and provide better results."*

> *"Fay, I'd appreciate your putting these files in alphabetical order for me so I can access them more easily."*

> *"Jean, would you come in a half hour early tomorrow morning, so we can set up the room and go over the agenda for the directors' meeting. I would feel more comfortable about the meeting if those things are taken care of ahead of time, so we can feel free to greet everyone as they arrive."*

These *conditional appreciation messages* contain the same three elements as appreciation messages, but they are based on the *condition* that a desired behavior will occur rather than on one that has already occurred. These conditional messages are recommended when the "difficult" person wants to do what pleases you but does not know what that is.

✍ Exercise 10: Conditional Appreciation Messages

Select one of the difficult behaviors you listed in Exercise 2. Using the guidelines for conditional appreciation messages, write a message asking the person to behave in the way you prefer.

_____
_____
_____

******

ENDNOTES

1. Kenneth Blanchard and Spencer Johnson, *The One Minute Manager* (New York: Berkley Books, 1982), 39.

2. Helen Hall Clinard, *Winning Ways to Succeed With People* (Houston, TX: Gulf Publishing, 1985) 5.

HOW TO DEAL WITH DIFFICULT PEOPLE

SUMMING IT UP

To summarize, "difficult people" often turn out not to be so difficult after all *if*

- you make an effort to change their behavior
- maintain a good working relationship
- examine your own contribution to the difficult behavior pattern
- are flexible in your communication modes
- encourage desirable behaviors

When you deal with a difficult person, remember this comment from a novel by Russian author Maxim Gorky:

> "Everybody, my friend, everybody lives for something better to come. That's why we want to be considerate of every man. Who knows what's in him, why he was born, and what he can do!"

Select from these Additional SkillPath Handbooks for Your Professional and Personal Growth

Title	Item Number
The Supervisor's Guide	12-0001
Power Write! A Practical Guide to Words that Work	12-0002
Every Woman's Guide to Career Success	12-0003
Taking Charge: A Personal Guide to Managing Projects and Priorities	12-0005
Meetings That Work	12-0006
Hiring and Firing: What Every Manager Needs to Know	12-0008

To order any of these resources, or to request a complete SkillPath Publications catalog, call toll-free **1-800-873-7545** or **1-913-362-3900.**